HOW TO
WRITE, PUBLISH, AND MARKET
Your First Book

The Ultimate Guide to Planning, Preparing, Writing, and Publishing Your First Book for Beginners!

DONIA YOUSSEF

The information and images contained in this book are protected under all Federal and International Copyright Laws and Treaties. Therefore, any use or reprint of the material in the book, either paperback or electronic, is prohibited. Users may not transmit or reproduce the material in any way, shape, or form – mechanically or electronically, such as recording, photocopying, or information storage and retrieval system – without getting prior written permission from the publisher/author.

All attempts have been made to verify the information contained in this book, "**How to Write, Publish, and Market Your First Book**" but the author and publisher do not bear any responsibility for errors or omissions. Any perceived negative connotation of any individual, group, or company is purely unintentional.

Furthermore, this book is intended as entertainment only, and as such, any and all responsibility for actions taken by reading this book lies with the reader alone and not with the author or publisher. This book is not intended as medical, legal, or business advice, and the reader alone holds sole responsibility for any consequences of any actions taken after reading this book.

Additionally, it is the reader's responsibility alone and not the author's or publishers to ensure that all applicable laws and regulations for the business practice are adhered to.

Copyright ©2020 Tiny Angel Press LTD.

All rights reserved. No part of this publication either writing or images may be reproduced, distributed, or transmitted in any form or by any means, including photocopying, recording, or other electronic or mechanical methods, without the prior written permission of the publisher, except in the case of brief quotations embodied in critical reviews and specific other non-commercial uses permitted by copyright law.

Published by **Tiny Angel Press LTD.**
Interior Formatting and Design: **Nonon Tech & Design**

ISBN: 978-1-8380713-6-3

DEDICATION

This book is dedicated to those
who wish to make a positive difference in their
life and the lives of others

TABLE OF CONTENTS

Introduction 1

Chapter 1: Commit to Writing Your Book 3
   Establish what your book is going to be about! 3
   Research your audience! 5
   Get new ideas for your book 6
   Do you have a dedicated writing space or area?..........7

Chapter 2: Decide What Type of Writer You Are 9
   What type of writer are you? The planner! 9
   Planning your book 10

Chapter 3: Budget for Self-Publishing Your Book 15
   How much are you willing to spend? 15
   Hiring a freelancer 18

Chapter 4: The Three Steps In Self-Publishing 19
   The different types of editing services available!..........20
   Formatting your book for ebook and
   paperback distribution 22
   Choosing where you're going to publish your book.....23
   Getting an ISBN for your book! 25

Chapter 5: Getting Ready to Publish Your Book 27
Writing an engrossing book title that sells! 27
Getting the perfect book cover for your book! 29
Writing a killer book description! 32
Building a launch team 34
Marketing Your Book 38

Chapter 6: Traditional Publishing, Hybrid Publishing, and Self-Publishing 43
What's the difference between traditional publishing, hybrid publishing, and self-publishing, and which is the best option for you and your book? 44
What is a literary agent, what do they do, and how can you find one? 47

Conclusion 51

References 53

INTRODUCTION

Writing a book isn't as straight forward as many people believe, but that doesn't mean that it must be as hard as some people make it. The more you plan, the easier it will go. Once you take the time to plan out your book, the entire process is going to run much smoother.

In the following book, we're going to take a detailed look at the steps you'll need to follow to plan, write, and publish a book successfully.

The first chapter is going to cover planning. Choosing a topic to write about, researching your audience, and who you're writing the book. Don't be afraid to pick a few different issues before you settle on your preferred topic. Think about where you're going to write your book and how much time you'll need to write it.

In the second chapter, we're going to look at what type of writer you are. Do you like to create a detailed outline, create character profiles, plan every chapter, or are you a pantser? Do you just grab your topic and run with it?

The focus of the third chapter is planning and budgeting. If you've never written a book, you might be surprised at how expensive they can be when you do them correctly.

We'll look at how much research you need to do, how long it's going to take you to write it and setting yourself achievable writing goals.

The fourth chapter looks at the three most essential steps in self-publishing, editing, proofreading, and formatting. This is where we'll look at different editing styles and formatting styles. We'll also take a quick look at how much they're going to cost and the pros and cons of doing it yourself.

When it comes to getting your book into the hands of readers, it all comes down to promotions and marketing. In the marketing chapter, we'll focus on marketing and the final touches on your manuscript. We'll look at the cover, choosing a title, building a launch team, marketing, and advertising for your new release.

The final chapter of the book will focus on, which is the best publishing option for you and your book. We'll take a closer look at traditional publishing, hybrid publishers, and self-publishing options for your manuscript or book.

All going well, by the time that you finish reading this book, you'll have an excellent blueprint for how your entire book process will go from conception to completion. The world can always do with more people putting their thoughts down on paper, and even if you never sell a million copies of your book, then it doesn't mean that it's not a fantastic book.

CHAPTER 1:

COMMIT TO WRITING YOUR BOOK

Once you've decided to write a book, you need to commit to it. It's not as straightforward or as hard as you think if you do it right. It can seem daunting when you first start, but once you plan it all out, you're going to be surprised at how easy it is.

Jump into it without any planning, and your first book could be a disaster.

In chapter one, we'll be focussing on what happens before you even put pen to paper or finger to keyboard. This time is where you'll plan your book and how you write it when you write it, and how much you write.

Establish what your book is going to be about!

It may seem obvious when you're sitting back and thinking about it, but many people start writing without a clear idea of what their book is going to be about. If you have a distinct sense of what you want to write about, that's fantastic. However, if you're thinking about becoming a writer and creating a book, but you're not sure what you're going to write about, this part is for you!

Self-publishing is becoming an extremely popular way for many people to earn an extra income on top of what they already earn. There has been an explosion in self-published books around the world over the last few years.

A lot of people rush into their first book, and it's essential that you don't make the same mistake that many new authors make by rushing. You may think that you're saving time by taking shortcuts in your book, but ultimately it may come back to haunt you in bad reviews and negative feedback or testimonials.

The first part of the book writing process is choosing what your book is going to be about and having an obvious idea of what the content is going to be. If you have one idea that's great, but if you're trying to incorporate multiple concepts or ideas, it may be easier to split them up into separate books rather than squeezing them into one book that's too complicated.

If you have a clear idea of the book topic and where you're heading in the book, you're going to end up with a much better book at the end of it. Fiction books are more straightforward in this regard because you're writing a story that can twist and turn yet remain on topic.

Non-fiction books are a little more complicated. It's much easier to get off topic and start branching out into other areas that require more detail. If you don't cover them in enough detail, people will feel like you rushed or didn't explore the content enough.

Research Your Audience!

Who is your book for? It sounds like an easy question, but it's an especially important one. Get it wrong, and your book may end up sitting on shelves missing its actual audience.

If you know who it is that you're writing the book for, you're going to have a much better idea when it comes to creating the content. For example, if you're writing a children's book, then what age group is you writing for? This will give you a much clearer idea of the words and phrasing that you use throughout the book.

If you were writing a non-fiction book, are you writing it for experienced people in that field, or is it aimed at beginners just getting started? When you write, you need to remember who you're writing for. If the content is too technical, then beginners won't be able to follow it. Too basic, and experts aren't going to be interested in reading it.

Take the time to look at what is currently available in the genre and subject you're writing in and see what questions are most asked. For example, if you were writing a book about beekeeping, is there is an ongoing group of questions being asked about certain aspects of beekeeping? If so, then a book that answers those questions would likely be beneficial to people that are thinking about beekeeping or are currently beekeeping.

If you know and understand your audience and what they're looking for and write your book accordingly, you already have an audience waiting to read your book.

Get New Ideas For Your Book

This subject ties into what we previously spoke about when told you to research your audience and understand what they're looking for. Obviously, if you can come up with a new idea that's never been done before, you may have less competition and a high chance of success. Or there's a reason no one has written about that topic before and there's no interest.

There are no guarantees in writing and especially in books. Just because you write and market a great book, there's no guarantee that anyone is interested enough in buying it.

Try to do some research about different ideas before you commit to writing too much of the book. For some writers, this is a large part of their process. They don't have a specific idea; they just look for something that's trending or popular, and they jump on board and write a book about it. For them, this is how they make their income. Some ideas are going to stick; some won't.

However, for many other authors, their book is a dream which they have been waiting to write for years. They have the entire book planned out in their head, and they're ready to write. For these authors, writing is a passion, and simply writing and creating the book is the biggest reward. Of course, selling a million copies would be a massive bonus, but for them, they are creating a piece of art, a dream, their life ambition.

Basically, there are two types of writers. Those that are looking to make money out of writing and those that write because they love it. Which type are you?

Do you have a dedicated writing space or area?

You might be surprised at how much more writing you can get done if you have a dedicated, functional, and comfortable writing space in your home. If you're relying on getting a laptop out and setting it up every time that you feel like writing, you're always going to miss great opportunities.

If you set up somewhere specific to do your writing, you're going to be able to sit down whenever you feel like writing and just start typing away. You want to ensure that your writing space meets the following three essential requirements:

1. **Dedicated Space** – It's vital that you have a dedicated space where your journal, laptop, tablet, or computer is set up and ready to use. This will make it a lot easier to sit down whenever you feel like writing and just start. If you have to set up everything each time, it's going to be much harder to get into any sort of flow or rhythm.

2. **Functional Space** – Your writing space needs to be practical and suit your writing. If you need peace and quiet, then set up your writing area somewhere that's free of distractions. You need a space that has everything you need ready to go, such as reference books, inspirational books, a detailed outline, a whiteboard, and anything else that you'll need to get your book written.

3. **Comfortable Space** – You need to ensure that your writing space is suitable for an hour or a day. This may require getting a high-quality writing desk and a comfortable and ergonomic chair. Good lighting,

fresh air, and a window are always a great way to allow you to relax and be comfortable while you're spending hours writing.

When you have your writing space set up perfectly, you're going to find it that much easier to consistently write your book without distractions.

CHAPTER 2:
DECIDE WHAT TYPE OF WRITER YOU ARE

Deciding what type of writer you are is easily broken down into two types: planners and pantsers. There are those writers that spend as much if not more time planning their book than they do writing it, and then there are those writers that just open up their computer or laptop and start writing without any clear plan.

It doesn't matter what type you are if you get the job done. We don't want to push you into a kind of writing style that doesn't suit you. However, just because you're a pantser or planner, it doesn't mean that you can't change or learn. A little bit of both styles is probably one of the best paths to go down.

What Type of Writer Are You? The Planner!

Just like it sounds, a planner is going to plan every aspect of their book. Regardless of whether it's fiction or non-fiction, there are certain aspects of your book that you can prepare before you choose to begin writing.

Planning Your Book

Let's look at some of the things you could plan for a fiction book:

1. **The Summary** – Summarize your entire book in one sentence. Don't worry about the characters. Just write a one-sentence summary of your complete book. If you plan on shopping your book or novel around to traditional publishers, it's this sentence that will be the hook.
2. **The Description** – The next step is to take that one sentence and then expand it. You're aiming to get about 3-5 sentences in this description. Most novels use a three-act structure for the storytelling aspect of the book.
    a. **Act One** – This will introduce your characters to the reader and set the stage for whatever is going to happen throughout the book. It also establishes what timeline the book is set in.
    b. **Act Two** – The second act or middle helps you to develop the theme of your book as well as build on the main characters. It's essential to have a certain amount of tension or conflict here to keep the reader interested.
    c. **Act Three** – This is where your story needs to really kick it up a gear! It's the final part of the book and reaches the final climax. There's nothing wrong with leaving a cliff-hanger for a sequel, but some readers will hate you for it!

4. **The Characters** – It's essential to fully develop your characters as they are the heart and soul of your book. Every character should get their own summary which should include the following information:
   a. Their name.
   b. The part that they will play in the book.
   c. What their goals are in the book.
   d. What motivates them.
   e. What is the conflict preventing them from achieving their goal?
   f. Their epiphany or what they will learn and how they will change.
   g. Finish with a brief summary of the character.
4. **The Expansion** – Now, it's time to take the description that you wrote in step two and expand it even further. You should aim to make each of the sentences and turn them into a detailed paragraph. At the end of this expansion, you should have a description which is approximately a page.
5. **The Characters Return** – Now, we want to take another look at our characters. Write a one-page synopsis of each character from their viewpoint. The benefit of this is that it will allow you to get to know your characters more.
6. **Time to Plot Again** – Go pack to your one-page plot that we created in step four and start expanding on each of the paragraphs. You want to focus on the main plot, any sub-plots that you plan on introducing, and any flashbacks. You should end up with about a four-page summary at this point.

7. **Added Character Detail** – Now's the time to dig right into those characters. Create a profile for each character and include things like their birthday, physical description including hair color, eye color, weight, etc., history, hobbies, likes and dislikes, and what they do as a profession. Think about how your character is going to evolve throughout the story.
8. **Set the Scene** – Take the synopsis that you created in step six and start breaking down every scene that you'll need throughout the novel. Every scene should include what happens in the scene, which characters are telling the story, any tension or conflict points that will draw your reader into the next chapter.
9. **It's Time to Write** – Now, the real work begins! It's time to write your first draft. It can seem daunting, but with all your prior planning, it should flow quite easily.
10. **Second Draft** – Your book will never be perfect the first time around. It's time to take another look from the beginning. Put the book aside for a week and take a break. Once you're ready, read through it from the start and make any necessary changes. Try to focus on ensuring that you have tied up any loose ends or plot holes.

There you have it! You have a detailed and complete planning structure to help you write your book. If you take the time to plan it out, then the writing component of the story is going to be much easier than you think.

If you're more of a pantser, then there isn't much of anything to plan. Pantsers come up with an idea for a book, or a character, or a scene, and then they take it from there and start writing. For some writers, being a pantser is the only way that they enjoy writing, and they find it quite useful.

CHAPTER 3:
BUDGET FOR SELF-PUBLISHING YOUR BOOK

Assuming that you're writing your own book and not hiring a ghostwriter, the writing aspect of your book is going to cost you nothing except your time. In the following chapter, we're going to take a closer look at how much it's going to cost to self-publish your book.

Many self-published authors choose to take on a variety of the following tasks themselves to save money, but beware, if it doesn't look professional, it could hurt sales of your book.

HOW MUCH ARE YOU WILLING TO SPEND?

How much your book ultimately costs to self-publish will depend on two especially important factors:
1. The type of book you write and how long it is.
2. The level of services that you provide.

If you're just trying to get a book out there and you're not worried about the finished quality, you can do almost every aspect yourself using guides and tutorials. However, if you want to sell copies of your book and make some money, then your book is going to require a considerable investment.

Below are some average figures that a 60,000-word book will cost to take it from the writing stage to the ready to publish stage. Be aware that these figures can vary depending on the level of service that you choose to purchase. That old saying *'you get what you paid for'* proves right in most situations.

Editing
- Developmental Editing – £1,500 - £3,000
- Copy Editing – £1,000 - £2,000
- Proofing – £500 - £1,000

Cover Design
- £50 - £1000

Formatting
- £150 - £800

Marketing
- £30 - £1,000

As with all things you do, how much you spend on your book will depend on how long it is, how much you're willing to invest, and the types of services that you choose.

They say never judge a book by its cover, but many people will quickly and easily move pass a book that looks like someone designed it themselves. A catchy and professional cover will ensure that you're finished book looks fantastic.

The interior formatting of your book is what makes it look professional and ensures that your book complies with industry style guides. Yes! There are a lot of specific rules which govern how the interior of your book should look. Professional formatting will ensure that your headings, drop caps, interior décor, and pages and chapters all flow smoothly.

You can choose to self-publish and complete each aspect of your book yourself, and it could end up okay, but professionals turn an okay book into a fantastic one.

For example, if you choose to do your own marketing, then it's going to cost you nothing at all. The compromise is that truly professional book marketing could pay for itself. When you're doing your marketing yourself, you might not have the same industry connections that professionals will have.

There are thousands of professional companies online to choose from to help with every aspect of your book creation. It's essential to do your homework before choosing one and committing a lot of money. Check out their reviews and testimonial, Google the business, and see if anyone has had bad experiences with that company and speak to other authors about who they used.

The final option is freelancers. In the next section, we'll look at what freelancers are and what types of services they provide.

Hiring a Freelancer

What is a freelancer? A freelancer is someone that provides services without you having to go through a company. An entire industry has grown up around freelancers and the services that they provide. Many companies around the world are now switching to running 100% with freelancers rather than employees.

There are a variety of different freelancing platforms available which an aspiring author could take advantage of, including Fiverr, Upwork, and many more. All you do is create an account on one of the platforms and then search for the services that you require.

Different platforms work in different ways. For example, on Fiverr freelancers set up '*gigs*' which clients can purchase. On Upwork, you create the project, and then freelancers bid on your project. There are writers, editors, formatters, marketers, graphic designers, and just about everything you can imagine.

One of the good things about freelancers is that you're often getting a superior service without the added costs that a business would charge. As we spoke about with companies, you must take the time to ensure that the freelancer you're paying is professional and can deliver the services that you require. Check out their feedback and reviews and take the time to talk to them about your project before you start.

CHAPTER 4:
THE THREE STEPS IN SELF-PUBLISHING

The three main steps we're going to talk about in self-publishing your book is editing, formatting, and choosing where you're going to sell or publish your books. The first area that we're going to focus on is the different types of editing and what they entail.

You may not be aware, but they're actually quite a lot of different types of editing and steps involved in successfully getting your book edited. Apart from writing, editing is one of the most crucial parts of your book. A great editor can transform an ordinary book into a fantastic book.

There are several factors which you need to consider before you hire an editor. The first factor that you'll need to consider is the genre or type of book. Many editors specialize in specific genres, and choosing one that enjoys working with your genre is crucial.

Below are some questions you should consider before hiring an editor:
1. Are you at the end of the book or just getting started?
2. Is this the first book you've written in this genre?
3. Is this your final draft or a rough draft?

4. Are you looking for an editor for future projects, or is this a one-off?

Think about these questions before you set off to choose your editor.

The different types of editing services available!

1. Developmental Editing

The first type of editing that we're going to look at is known as developmental editing. A developmental editor can help flesh out ideas and shape your book before you get too committed to the current draft. A developmental editor is usually involved in your book right from the start of the project until its successful completion.

2. Manuscript Evaluation

Just like it sounds, a manuscript evaluation is a thorough evaluation of your book. If you get fantastic feedback from your editor, you might be able to move to the proofreading stage, but if it's the opposite, you may have quite a lot of work ahead of you. However, you need to be prepared for some honest and confronting feedback when you get a manuscript. A good editor will let you know if your book requires work, even if it's negative.

3. Line Editing

This is where your editor goes through your manuscript line by line. They will look at different aspects of your writing, including the flow, clarity, and tone of your book. Your editor will also look at things like run-on sentences, pacing, and clichés. Many editors will also correct grammar and punctuation during the line editing process.

4. Copy Editing

A lot of people disagree about how copy editing is different than proofing, but there are some differences. Your editor will look at spelling and grammar, but they'll also look at style rules and guidelines during the copyediting process. The two most common style guides are the Associated Press (AP) and the Chicago Manual.

5. Proofing

Believe it or not, but even after all this editing, your final manuscript will require proofreading. This is the final chance for you to correct any spelling mistakes and typos in your manuscript before it reaches the print stage, and you print off 1000 copies.

Formatting Your Book for Ebook and Paperback Distribution

When it comes to selling your book, you have several different options. You can do any single one of them or all of them. The two main types are digital copies, which are known as ebooks and physical copies of your book known as paperbacks. The other options are audiobooks, and then within the paperback category, you can choose from a variety of different styles, including hardcover, etc.

Ultimately the style or type of book you release will be up to you and how you intend on selling your book in the future.

When it comes to formatting, different platforms will have different requirements. Wherever you intend on selling your book, be it Amazon, Smashwords, iBooks, Ingram Spark, Kobo, Barnes, and Noble, you'll need to check what their specific guidelines are. The same applies if you're planning on printing your own books through a printer. They will have particular requirements which you'll need to meet.

We can't recommend professional formatting more! Your formatter will be aware of different platform's requirements and the different style rules which apply to both ebooks and paperbacks. It's the formatting that will ultimately give your book a professional look and feel and plays a massive role in the enjoyment people get when they read your book.

Bad formatting or unprofessional formatting can quickly turn into bad reviews and feedback from readers and need to be avoided at all costs, especially when you're just getting started and trying to build up a reputation as a new author.

Choosing where you're going to publish your book

When it comes to where you self-publish your book, you would be surprised at how many options there are out there to choose from. It's vital that you consider your options before you commit to one platform, as some platforms require you to be exclusive with them.

In the following section, we'll take a closer look at some of the more popular self-publishing platforms and what each of them has to offer.

Amazon KDP

One of the undeniably biggest self-publishing platforms available is Amazon KDP. There's a reason so many authors choose to go with Amazon, and it's because of their massive distribution range. KDP is where you'll head to self-publish your book, and the uploading and set up procedure is quite straightforward and easy to follow. Uploading your books on Amazon is 100% free, and you can make as many edits to your book as you like.

You can choose to set up either an ebook, paperback or both. When you upload your ebook, you'll be asked whether or not you want to take part in Kindle Unlimited (KU).

KU will allow you to get five free days every ninety-days, or price reduction promotions. People that have KU can read your book for free. However, you get compensated at the end of the month with a price per page read, which comes out of the KU pool of resources.

The negative side of enrolling in KU is that you can't make your ebook available on any other platform. It has to be exclusive with KU and Amazon for the ninety-day enrollment period. You can enroll your paperbacks on other platforms, but the ebook must be exclusive to KU.

KU will allow you to create an author profile on Amazon and will also link all of your books together under your author name. As you release new books and add them to Amazon, they'll all be linked together for everyone to find. Amazon has stores set up in almost every region and country in the world, and it's a great way to make your book available to multiple places all at once.

With paperbacks, you have two options. You can do Print On Demand (POD), where Amazon prints and ships your book every time you sell one or drop ship your books directly to Amazon. You'll need to handle all the printing and shipping, but every time that someone buys a book, it will ship from Amazon.

Ingram Spark

Ingram Spark is similar to Amazon in that they list your ebook and paperback, but with one significant difference. They don't have a platform where people browse books; instead, they put your book on different platforms, including Amazon,

Barnes, and Noble, and iBooks. Ingram Spark also has a lot of reach into libraries and schools through its newsletter and book catalog options.

One advantage that Ingram Spark has is that they can send your book to multiple platforms (you select which ones you want), and they have a variety of different printing options for paperbacks. You can have hardcover options as well as a variety of different paper and color choices.

It's essential that you have your file files polished before uploading them to Ingram Spark as there is both a setup fee as well as a fee to make changes to your file.

Smashwords

Smashwords is like both Amazon and Ingram Spark combining elements of both platforms into one. You can distribute your books to multiple other platforms, and they also have an established sales platform where people can browse and buy paperbacks and ebooks. They can also help you to add your ebooks to other platforms such as iBooks and Barnes and Noble.

Getting an ISBN for your book!

When you upload your book to Amazon KU, you necessarily require an ISBN, as Amazon will assign an ASIN number for you. However, if you plan on publishing your books on multiple book platforms, having your own ISBN is an absolute must.

If you live in the United States and the United Kingdom, you must purchase your ISBNs. The more you buy at once, the cheaper it is, but once assigned to a book, an ISBN cannot be edited or changed, and ever can the title or subtitle of the book.

Some countries, such as Canada, will allow you to obtain your ISBNs for free. However, you must send a physical copy of your book to the Canadian Book Library.

What is an ISBN? An International Standard Book Number (ISBN) is a 13-digit number that is used to identify a specific book. The ISBN allows people to differentiate between your text and one of the millions of other books available around the world, even if they have the same title.

You need to be 100% sure that you're happy with your book title and sub-title before registering your ISBN as it can't be changed later. Your ISBN is displayed along with your barcode and listed on all the publishing information when you publish your book.

CHAPTER 5:

GETTING READY TO PUBLISH YOUR BOOK

By this stage of your book, you should be looking at the publishing stage and preparing everything for the final release of your book to the public. It's essential that you don't get over-excited at this stage and rush to release your book before it's 100% completed.

In the following chapter, we're going to look at choosing and creating a catchy title, getting the perfect cover, building a launch team for your book, marketing your book, and how to write an excellent book description that will help you sell books.

Skipping even one of these steps can mean the difference between selling a few books and a few thousand books, so take your time and don't rush through them in the excitement of releasing a book!

Writing An Engrossing Book Title That Sells!

Choosing a catchy book title is a crucial part of your book. With fiction books, the title is a little easier to come up with because it should relate to the content or genre of the book. Try to choose something exciting and look back to your one-line summary that we created earlier in the book during the development and planning chapter.

Below, we have some great tips for helping you choose the perfect non-fiction book title. It's important to remember that keywords come into play when you're thinking of your book title, and relevant keywords should be incorporated where possible into your book title.

- » Good titles are focussed on your audience – Bad titles are focussed on you or your product.
- » Good titles are short, clear, and strong – Bad titles are weak, confusing, and too long.
- » Good titles solve a problem – Bad titles sell a solution.
- » Good titles connect with readers on an emotional level – Bad titles miss their audience completely.
- » Good titles are easy to remember – Bad titles are quickly forgotten.

Rules for Creating the Perfect Non-Fiction Book Title

1. Always address the book title towards a single person. You never want to try to appeal to a group of people. Instead, try to focus on creating a title that appeals to the person holding your book in their hand so that it appeals to them.
2. What does your audience want? What are they searching for? Try to create a book title that appeals to your audience's desires.
3. The title of your book is supposed to sell the idea of your book to your audience, and it must do it quickly. You only have a second to make someone choose your book over the millions of other books available.

Once you have come up with a list of book names that you love, try getting some feedback from beta readers or other authors if you're part of an author group. Ask them which titles and sub-titles they prefer and why? You should be able to get a pretty clear idea of what's working with your book title and what areas need more work.

Getting the Perfect Book Cover for Your Book!

They say that you should never judge a book by its cover, but a large percentage of readers choose books with their eyes first. Once you're a recognized author with a dedicated group of readers, you'll be able to get away with creating more original ideas for covers. Still, when you first start, you need to create a book cover that instantly appeals to readers.

Getting a professional book cover designed can be a substantial investment, but the returns on that investment make it well worth it. There are a variety of professional book cover designers available to choose from, each with their packages and options. Ultimately, whichever one you choose should suit you, your book, and your budget.

When you get a cover designed through a professional cover designer, they'll ask you several questions about your book, including the genre, the style you like, what you're looking for out of your cover, and also if you have any cover designs that you like. The designer will then use this information to come up with several draft sketches, and you'll go from there.

It's crucial that you go into the cover design process with an open mind. Remember, they are professional and have helped design thousands of covers. Often, as authors, we get tunnel vision on specific ideas, and it's hard to look past them when someone is trying to offer us something different.

Another great tip that we recommend is asking for the original files or design files. If you ever want to make a change to your cover and your designer is missing in action, you'll have the design file available to give to another designer.

Designing Your Own Book Cover in Seven Easy Steps

If designing your own book cover is your only option because of budget restraints, then here are some simple steps and guidelines to follow. You need to remember that any book cover is a balance between images, text, and information. It's the first thing that a potential reader will see and often means the difference between someone picking it up or passing it by.

Seven Simple Steps for Designing Your Own Book Cover!

1. **Look for inspiration** – You first stop in finding inspiration is to check out the competition. Look at what other books in your genre have done and whether they're selling. You don't have to make your cover the same, but it should give you some inspiration for a direction to head in.

2. **Use professional software** – Photoshop and InDesign by Adobe are probably the best two programs that anyone can use to design a cover. There are thousands of free tutorials online, which will allow you to master some of the most complicated steps in cover design.
3. **Premium images** – If you're going to use any photos, make sure they're a minimum of 300dpi. You can buy pictures from places such as Shutterstock, and there are also free stock images available. Be aware. Some stock images require you to pay a licensing fee if you plan on using them for a book cover or product.
4. **Create a cover that suits your dimensions** – A great cover is no good to you if it doesn't meet your required specifications. Every platform or printer will have template guidelines for you to follow. The size of your cover needs to match the size of your formatted file, and the finished page count will give you the size of your spine.
5. **Typography is critical** – Check out how professional publishing companies have used typography on their covers. It's crucial to find the right balance between the fonts and styles you use and your cover design. Also, you don't need to include written by or a novel by. Your readers can figure that bit out themselves!
6. **File type** – Make sure that you export or save your files in the correct format for uploading or printing. Always keep the original file type in case you need to go back and make any changes later.

7. **Feedback** – Feedback is an absolute must. Take your draft cover to a group of friends, readers, authors, or family members and get their opinion. It's easy as an author to fall in love with a cover and get tunnel vision about how effective it's going to be. The last thing that you want is a cover that you love, but all your readers hate.

It's important to remember that your book cover is a marketing tool for the sale and promotion of your book and is a lot more than just the cover. It's going to feature in every promotion that you do and every advertisement. You need to ensure that you have a book cover that you love but also one that any potential reader is going to fall in love with too.

Writing a Killer Book Description!

After your cover and title, the next thing that's going to sell your book is your book description, and you need to make sure that it's perfect. Similar to your cover, you only have a few seconds to convince a reader that they need your book and should purchase it.

When you first start out as an author, your cover, your title, and your book description are doing a lot of the heavy lifting in the sales department. With so many books available for people to buy, you need to ensure that yours stands out. It's hard to compete against James Patterson or J. K. Rowling, so you need to give your readers a reason to take a chance on an unknown author.

This is where your description plays a significant role. In the following section, we're going to look at some great tips for writing a killer book description for your book!

1. **Keep it simple** – Your book description doesn't need to be another novel. Your cover is only so big, and there are a limited number of words that you're going to be able to fit on it. You should aim to have two versions of your book description. One for your back cover and one for the description space on whatever online platform you're selling your book on. The back-cover description should be about 100-150 words. Your online description can be longer, approximately 250 words, and should also include relevant keywords based on the topic and genre of your book.

2. **Catchy heading** – The heading of your book description should tell people the most important thing about the book, what they're going to learn, what problem you're solving, or why they should read this book over other books. You need your reader to be instantly attracted to your book in one sentence. Think back to your one-line summary of your book.

3. **Introduce your book** – The next part of the description should introduce the reader to the book, what they're going to learn, or get from the book, the main characters.

4. **Call to action** – A call to action is a phrase which induces a reader to take action. For example, download this book now if you want to learn everything there is to know about self-publishing. You should include a call

to action in the first section. Try to have it somewhere that readers will be able to see without having to scroll further down the page.

5. **Include HTML** – If you're creating a book description for your online book description, then you can include HTML, such as **bolds**, *italics*, and <u>underlines</u>. You can also use larger headings and bullet-points throughout the description. These will help to highlight key areas of your description and make your description stand out.

Excellent book descriptions not only help sell your book, but they will also help with search rankings on online platforms such as Amazon. With so many different books available for readers to choose, any little boost that gets your book ahead of another author is going to help.

BUILDING A LAUNCH TEAM

As a new author, you're probably already dreaming of the ultimate launch team helping you to sell and market your book. Or you think I'll be able to handle it all myself, no worries. The truth is a bit of both. There is a lot of work to be done whenever you launch a new book, and the marketing and social media aspect of book releases can quickly become overwhelming for many new authors.

One of the most effective ways to ensure that your new book release is getting the marketing attention that it deserves is to create what's known as a book launch team. For many readers, being part of a book launch team is an exciting and fun time. They get early access to a book that no one else has access to, and it's exciting for them. They'll be able to tell their friends about it, and they'll want to join in too! As you build up more of a following as an author, this power will increase, and so to will the number of people that want to take part.

The tricky part is getting the entire process started. How do you find all these fantastic people willing to read and review your book, create posts about it, tell their friends, etc.? To help make creating your book launch team building a little easier, we have seven steps below that will speed up the process and ensure that your launch team has the best chance of success!

1. **Recruit on social media** – Never underestimate the power of social media. If you're planning on releasing a book and you have social media pages such as Facebook, Instagram, or Twitter setup, then reach out to your followers. If they're following your page, there is a good chance that they're already interested in your book.
2. **Use your email list** – If you have an email list for subscribers, then send out an email. You want your book launch team to be as big as you can potentially manage, but you don't want it to seem open and available to everyone. Creating some demand by using phrases like limited numbers or first to apply will help to reach those that are the most eager to take part.
3. **Don't wait until a week before** – You need to start this process at least 1-2 months before the release date of your book. Getting it all organized and dealing with multiple people is going to take a lot of time, especially

if you're doing it yourself. This is also where a personal assistant could come in handy. There are lots of PAs online that help authors out for a reasonable price.

4. **Create an effective way to communicate** – Facebook groups and chats are useful for talking, but all that talking quickly dilutes the message and any instructions. Creating an email list with your book launch team and sending out accurate and up-to-date instructions is the easiest way to avoid any miscommunications.

5. **Send out Advanced Reader Copies** – ARCs are the best way to create a buzz in advance, and it serves two purposes. Not only is your launch team excited to get a physical book, but they'll also proofread your book for you at the same time. You will get a lot of feedback about any issues, typos, or mistakes well in advance, and you can edit your master book file before the hard release. You should establish early how your book launch team can send you any errors and give them a specific You want to have your ARC copies arrive 2-3 weeks before the launch of your book. This gives your launch team enough time to read the book and write a review and get anything promotional ready. If you do it too soon, you risk people losing interest.

6. **Specify what you're looking for** – You need to specify what you expect out of your launch team before you recruit them. Let them know that you expect social media posts, reviews, testimonials, pre-orders, or whatever it is you would like before you send out ARC copies. This way, everyone knows where they stand

and is ready to leap into action on the day of release. Most experts recommend the following:
- » Post a review to Amazon and other online platforms such as iBooks, Barnes & Noble, Goodreads, Google, or Smashwords.
- » Pre-order a copy of the book or buy a copy for a friend.
- » Share posts on social media such as Instagram, Twitter, or Facebook with pre-discussed hashtags.
- » Share the book release on blogs. (If they have them).

7. **Reward your launch team** – This is an essential step if you want to continue growing and using your launch team. Remember to thank them and reward them for putting so much effort into your book launch. There are a variety of different ways that you can thank people, including a personal Q & A video session, autographed hard copies of your book, gift cards, and gift vouchers, personalized thank you emails, and advanced copies of special releases or content.

If you do it right, your book launch team can be one of the most beneficial and special marketing tools that you possess as an author. Treat them special, reward them, and watch your book launch team continue to grow and grow.

Hopefully, with the use of these seven tips, you'll be able to create a fantastic book launch team for your next book launch. One of the greatest things about book launch teams is that they create an immense amount of organic buzz when you first release your book. This early spike in sales will help to increase the rank of your book and push further sales.

Marketing Your Book

When it comes to marketing your book, you have several different options, and most of them are going to depend on how much you're willing to invest. As we discussed above, a book launch team is a fantastic way to create marketing buzz around the release of your book, but they take time to organize.

There is no magic amount of money to spend or marketing strategy that's going to guarantee that you sell a million dollars worth of books. If there were, we'd all be doing it! For some authors, they do absolutely no marketing and manage to hit a book out of the park. For others, they spend thousands of dollars on marketing and never see their investment paid back.

The good news is that there are a variety of different things that you can do yourself that aren't going to break the bank. Below, we'll look at some of the different ways that you can market your book that isn't going to cost you a fortune.

Social Media Pages

The first and most obvious way to market your book, which is 100% free and is only going to cost you time, is social media. The leading platforms that authors are using are Facebook,

Instagram, Twitter, and LinkedIn. You can create posts, book groups, and just about anything else you can imagine. We recommend that you create an author account separate from your personal account so that you can keep your professional and personal life separate. This is a lot easier if you're using a pen name. If you're publishing books under your own name, you need to be vigilant about what you post on your personal social media accounts as the two are easily linked. You can also incorporate paid posts or boosted posts on social media. You need to post something first, and then you can go through and set a budget for how much you would like to spend boosting your post. These paid posts usually have a click through to purchase your book, like your post, share your post, or follow your page. The beauty of social media is that you can put as much or as little as you want into it.

Join Book Related Groups

Places like Goodreads, AllAuthor, Book Bub, and Book Works are all platforms where authors can create profiles and list their books. Some websites are targeted towards readers, while others are great places for authors and readers to connect with each other. Whenever you join sites and groups, you must follow the group rules. Some groups are happy for authors to promote their books, while others aren't and have special days and events for authors.

Contact your local bookstores and libraries

Author signings and author reading are great opportunities to connect with local readers in your area. You would be surprised at how many schools, libraries, bookstores, and other locations are happy to have an author come and do a reading of their book. These readings and events are also a fantastic opportunity for you to create content for your social media pages.

Send out ARC copies of your books for reviewers

As an author, you generally have access to much cheaper copies of your books. Sending out ARC copies of books or physical copies of books for people to review or do social media features in your book is a great way to create a buzz about your book. It also ties back into your social media and marketing. When you send out physical copies of your book, you can include promotional material.

Create promotional material to giveaway

When you handle all your book shipping or send out ARC copies of books, it's an excellent opportunity to add in other promotional material. You can create short stories, bookmarks, postcards, pamphlets, and so much more! The only thing limiting you is your own creativity and imagination.

Guest posts on blogs, vlogs, and podcasts

Another great way to market your book is to do guest posts on other people's blogs, vlogs, and podcasts. As well as doing author interviews, features, and take over events, you can generally include links to your books and social media platforms. These posts are almost always 100% free and allow you to offer the same opportunity to other people to guest post on your website in exchange.

Hopefully, with the tips and ideas we have given you above, you'll be all set to get started marketing your book! Don't be dismayed by poor results. There are no guarantees in marketing and self-publishing but if you get it right, the rewards can be fantastic!

CHAPTER 6:
TRADITIONAL PUBLISHING, HYBRID PUBLISHING, AND SELF-PUBLISHING

When it comes time to release your book out into the wild and to publish it, you actually three options or paths that you can follow as an author. Each of the three options has its own advantages and disadvantages, and ultimately, it's going to be up to you as the writer and author to choose a publishing path that suits your requirements.

The three choices you have are:
1. Self-publishing your book yourself as the author and publisher.
2. Submitting your book to a traditional publishing company and having them publish your book on your behalf.
3. Working with a hybrid publisher to release your book.

In the next section of this chapter, we're going to take a look at each of your three options and the advantages and disadvantages of each of them so that you'll be able to make a more educated decision about which choice is the best fit for you and your book.

What's the difference between traditional publishing, hybrid publishing, and self-publishing, and which is the best option for you and your book?

Self-Publishing

The first option that we're going to look at is self-publishing. As we have spoken about throughout the book, self-publishing is where you take care of every aspect of publishing your book, including writing, illustrating, editing, formatting, cover, publishing, and marketing.

The advantages of self-publishing are that you retain 100% of the rights to your book, and you receive 100% of any royalties. You also have full control over how much you market your book and where you sell it.

The disadvantages to self-publishing are that you're responsible for every aspect of your book and every cost associated with it. If it succeeds or fails is ultimately up to you and what you put into it. The learning curve associated with self-publishing can be steep and expensive, but extremely rewarding if you master it and get it right.

Traditional Publishing

Traditional publishing like the name suggests is when you write a great book, and a publishing company pays you to write it, and then they publish it on your behalf. Most famous authors you know and read all publish their books through traditional publishing houses.

The advantages to traditional publishing are that you get paid a certain amount for your book upfront and then receive a percentage of all the royalties that the book earns as long as it's under contract with the publisher. You can choose to keep extending your agreement with the publisher, or when the contract is finished, you can take back the rights to your book. It means that your publisher will take care of each step in the publishing process and marketing process. You are paying for every part of the publishing process along the way. Ultimately, if the book isn't a success, you'll still receive your agreed-upon payment amount.

The disadvantages of traditional publishing are that it's not easy to get a book published. Some authors write for their entire life and never receive a book deal. You need to find yourself a literary agent, and that can be a complicated process in itself. When you sign a contract with a publishing company, you lose control of your book, and it's up to them what they do with it. They may choose not to publish after you write it, and you'll need to wait several years before you can receive the rights to your book back.

Traditional publishers also receive a large percentage of the royalties, especially when you first get started, and you're an unknown author. After all, they're paying you and investing in your book, so they need to get something back from the deal.

Hybrid Publishing

The final option we are going to talk about is a blend between self-publishing and traditional publishing known as hybrid publishing or vanity publishing. Now, hybrid publishing doesn't have the best reputation among authors, and there is a reason why. Hybrid publishing is essentially where you pay the publisher to publish your book.

You're going to have to pay for the development of the book, publishing, and marketing. At the end of the process, they will publish your book and do the agreed-upon amount of publishing, but they'll also take a percentage of your royalties.

Many new authors fall into the trap of working with hybrid publishers. Hybrid publishers basically do all the steps you would need to do as a self-published author and charge you for it. If you are approached by a company about publishing your book, it's always a good idea to do a thorough background check of them first before you agree to sign any contracts.

Speak to other authors in your author circle, do some internet searches of the company, and have the contract examined by a lawyer. Don't rush in and sign anything without taking the time to thoroughly understand what it is you're agreeing to and always be wary if you're asked to pay for anything yourself or hand over any money.

What is a Literary Agent, What Do They Do, and How Can You Find One?

A literary agent represents you as an author and helps mediate a publishing deal between you and a publishing company. A literary agent can also represent you if a film, theatre, or television studio wants to turn your book into a movie, television show, or play. They work off a fee and help to negotiate the best deal for you.

Below, we'll look at some of the advantages and disadvantages of hiring and working with a literary agent.

Advantages to Working With a Literary Agent:

1. A great literary agent helps you as an author get new opportunities, and generally, they have some excellent industry connections that regular people don't have access to. They will handle all aspects of the contract negotiations and any publicity events on your behalf.
2. A great literary agent will be able to offer insight and suggestions on your manuscript before you send it off to publishers. Agents understand what publishers are looking for and will help their clients put their best work forward.
3. A great literary agent will prepare all your query letters and pitch packages. They'll help you choose what you send to publishers and keep track of all the submissions.

Finding a good literary agent can be like winning the lottery. There are plenty out there, but there is also a lot of demand from new authors that are looking for deals. Sure, you could try and pitch your book or manuscript yourself, but most of the large publishing companies won't even look at unsolicited pitches or work with new authors. A literary agent is your best chance of cutting through the red tape and getting your ideas in front of the right people.

Once you have an agent, you can focus more on writing and less on trying to sell your books. They'll take the stress and hard work out of pitching your new books and help guide your career as an author.

That doesn't mean that all literary agents are fantastic, and there are some disadvantages to working with a literary agent.

Disadvantages to Working With a Literary Agent:

1. **Trust** – You need to have 100% trust in your agent as they are going to be handling the financial side of your business. One way that you can confirm that your agent is reputable is if they're a member of the Association of Authors' Representatives (AAR), an organization with a searchable database whose signatories promise to observe an ethical code of conduct when representing clients. There is always a risk with any agent you work with, but if you take the time to do your research thoroughly, you'll be less likely to get stuck with a dishonest agent.

2. **Cost** – You're going to have to pay your agent. Agents generally work based on a commission from their authors. Try to avoid any agent that charges you fees upfront just to read your manuscript. Most literary agents take a commission between 10-20%. If you don't like the sound of handing over that much money, then self-publishing may be a better option for you rather than publishing.
3. **Time** – They may slow down the process of getting your book published. Every step in the publishing process takes time, and adding a literary agent into the process will make it even longer. If you are in a hurry to see some money or see your book published, having a literary agent will slow down that process. It can take anywhere from twelve months to twenty-four months by the time you go through the entire process.

How Can You Find a Literary Agent?

Finding a literary agent is like finding the perfect person to marry. It all depends on you and what you have to offer. It's important to remember that literary agents are chasing authors around looking for new clients. It is the other way around. You're going to have to work extremely hard to get a good agent and just as hard to get your book published.

Below we have some great places where you can research and look for potential literary agents. Don't be dismayed if you get rejected as there are no guarantees, and many agents already have a long list of clients, and they aren't looking for any new authors.

- » **Publishers Marketplace** – This is the best place for you to research literary agents because many agents have member pages there, and you can also search the publishing deals database by genre, category, and keyword. This will allow you to pinpoint the best agents for your style of writing or book.
- » **Agent Query** – There are about 1,000 agent listings on agent query, and it is a great community and resource for any writers that are currently going through the query process to join and become a part of.
- » **Query Tracker** – There are about 200 publishers listed on Query Tracker and also over a thousand agent listings for you to check out.
- » **Writers Market** – There are approximately 400 to 600 agent listings on Writers Market, but there is also a monthly subscription fee.
- » **The Guide to Literary Agents** – This is a fantastic blog, but it's also an excellent resource for news and views related to literary agents and the publishing world.

As with anything related to publishing, there are no guarantees, and the process of getting an agent and dealing with publishers can be time-consuming and emotionally draining. Many authors start off looking for publishers and agents but end up self-publishing their own books.

CONCLUSION

Thanks for reading this book on writing, publishing, and selling your first book. Hopefully, with the knowledge that you have gained, you're going to be in a much better position to plan, write, market, and sell your book.

The greatest thing about writing and publishing your very own book is that you have created something that will be around forever. You can print a copy of your book and hold it in your hands and read the words that you have created.

For many authors, the act of writing and publishing their book is an essential part of their life, and they aren't worried if they never sell a copy. Sure, it's great if people buy it, but just creating it is the best part of the journey.

If you are planning on writing and selling books with the intention of selling them, then put 100% of you into it. Invest in books that teach you what you aren't sure about. Learn from other authors that have succeeded and failed. Learn from what they did right and what they did wrong and how you can avoid it.

Invest in yourself and your book as if it's a business. If you only put 50% into your books, then how are you ever expecting to get 100% back out? You never will. Pay for a professional cover, get a professional editor, and a professional formatter.

Look at marketing options. You never know how well your book is going to go until you put everything you have into it.

There are no guarantees in life, and there are none in writing, but at the end of the day, it can be an exceptionally emotionally rewarding process. Have fun with writing, and you might just find yourself at a book signing one day with thousands of readers waiting to get your autograph!

All the world's best authors started out just where you are right now with an idea for a book that they love and the inspiration to go after their dreams. So, stop thinking about writing your book and get started writing it! It's not going to write itself, and you'll never know if you have that bestseller inside you until you write it and publish it.

Happy writing!

REFERENCES

How To Write A Book
https://jerryjenkins.com/how-to-write-a-book/

10 Steps To Planning A Book
https://www.writersbureau.com/writing/planning-a-novel.htm

How Much Does it Cost To Self-Publish
https://blog.reedsy.com/cost-to-self-publish-a-book/

Different Types of Editing
https://www.clearvoice.com/blog/types-of-editors/

The Best Self-Publishing Platforms for your Book
https://www.authorservicesaustralia.com.au/2020/05/25/self-publishing-platforms/

What Is An ISBN
https://www.isbn.org/faqs_general_questions

Writing the Perfect Book Title
https://cascadiaauthorservices.com/book-titles/

Creating the Perfect Book Cover
https://blog.reedsy.com/book-cover-design/

Tips For Writing A Great Book Description
https://www.indiepublishinggroup.com/tips-writing-great-book-description/

Building a Launch Team
https://www.startawildfire.com/2018/05/6-steps-to-build-a-dynamic-book-launch-team.html

10 Ways to Promote Your Book
https://www.draft2digital.com/blog/10-low-or-no-budget-ways-to-promote-your-book/

Three Types of Publishing
https://allthekissing.com/2018/12/3-types-of-publishing-traditional-indie-and-hybrid/

What is a Literary Agent? Pros and Cons
https://www.masterclass.com/articles/pros-and-cons-of-hiring-a-literary-agent

Association of Authors' Representatives (AAR)
http://aaronline.org/

Where Can you Find a Literary Agent?
https://www.janefriedman.com/find-literary-agent/

Printed in Great Britain
by Amazon